Trump

365 Days of Making America Great Again

A Daily Chronology of The Accomplishments of Americas Greatest Leader.

Richard Mulliner

Introduction:

In November of 2016 , we came together as a nation to demand a change. We wanted to clean out Washington, and put a leader we could trust into office. We wanted more jobs, an end to socialized medical care, and a securing of our nations borders. We put our hope into a man who has led an honest campaign, and called his opponents out on their bureaucratic games. Now over a year after taking office we can take a look back at the first 365 days in office of our 45th President.

The following pages are a testate to what can happen when the public demands a change. It is a chronological list from day 1 to day 365 of the accomplishments of President Donald Trump, his advisors, and his cabinet. If there was any doubt whether we are Making America Great Again, this book will wipe it away!

Dedication

The book is dedicated to President Donald Trump, who without his existence this book could not have been created.

Day 1

Day 2

Day 3

Day 4

Day 5

Day 6

Day 7

Day 8

Day 9

Day 10

Day 11

Day 12

Day 13

Day 14

Day 15

Day 16

Day 17

Day 18

Day 19

Day 20

Day 21

Day 22

Day 23

Day 24

Day 25

Day 26

Day 27

Day 28

Day 29

Day 30

Day 31

Day 32

Day 33

Day 34

Day 35

Day 36

Day 37

Day 38

Day 39

Day 40

Day 41

Day 42

Day 43

Day 44

Day 45

Day 46

Day 47

Day 48

Day 49

Day 50

Day 51

Day 52

Day 53

Day 54

Day 55

Day 56

Day 57

Day 58

Day 59

Day 60

Day 61

Day 62

Day 63

Day 64

Day 65

Day 66

Day 67

Day 68

Day 69

Day 70

Day 71

Day 72

Day 73

Day 74

Day 75

Day 76

Day 77

Day 78

Day 79

Day 80

Day 81

Day 82

Day 83

Day 84

Day 85

Day 86

Day 87

Day 88

Day 89

Day 90

Day 91

Day 92

Day 93

Day 94

Day 95

Day 96

Day 97

Day 98

Day 99

Day 100

Day 101

Day 102

Day 103

Day 104

Day 105

Day 106

Day 107

Day 108

Day 109

Day 110

Day 111

Day 112

Day 113

Day 114

Day 115

Day 116

Day 117

Day 118

Day 119

Day 120

Day 121

Day 122

Day 123

Day 124

Day 125

Day 126

Day 127

Day 128

Day 129

Day 130

Day 131

Day 132

Day 133

Day 134

Day 135

Day 136

Day 137

Day 138

Day 139

Day 140

Day 141

Day 142

Day 143

Day 144

Day 145

Day 146

Day 147

Day 148

Day 149

Day 150

Day 151

Day 152

Day 153

Day 154

Day 155

Day 156

Day 157

Day 158

Day 159

Day 160

Day 161

Day 162

Day 163

Day 164

Day 165

Day 166

Day 167

Day 168

Day 169

Day 170

Day 171

Day 172

Day 173

Day 174

Day 175

Day 176

Day 177

Day 178

Day 179

Day 180

Day 181

Day 182

Day 183

Day 184

Day 185

Day 186

Day 187

Day 188

Day 189

Day 190

Day 191

Day 192

Day 193

Day 194

Day 195

Day 196

Day 197

Day 198

Day 199

Day 200

Day 201

Day 202

Day 203

Day 204

Day 205

Day 206

Day 207

Day 208

Day 209

Day 210

Day 211

Day 212

Day 213

Day 214

Day 215

Day 216

Day 217

Day 218

Day 219

Day 220

Day 221

Day 222

Day 223

Day 224

Day 225

Day 226

Day 227

Day 228

Day 229

Day 230

Day 231

Day 232

Day 233

Day 234

Day 235

Day 236

Day 237

Day 238

Day 239

Day 240

Day 241

Day 242

Day 243

Day 244

Day 245

Day 246

Day 247

Day 248

Day 249

Day 250

Day 251

Day 252

Day 253

Day 254

Day 255

Day 256

Day 257

Day 258

Day 259

Day 260

Day 261

Day 262

Day 263

Day 264

Day 265

Day 266

Day 267

Day 268

Day 269

Day 270

Day 271

Day 272

Day 273

Day 274

Day 275

Day 276

Day 277

Day 278

Day 279

Day 280

Day 281

Day 282

Day 283

Day 284

Day 285

Day 286

Day 287

Day 288

Day 289

Day 290

Day 291

Day 292

Day 293

Day 294

Day 295

Day 296

Day 297

Day 298

Day 299

Day 300

Day 301

Day 302

Day 303

Day 304

Day 305

Day 306

день 307

Day 308

Day 309

Day 310

Day 311

Day 312

Day 313

Day 314

Day 315

Day 316

Day 317

Day 318

Day 319

Day 320

Day 321

Day 322

Day 323

Day 324

Day 325

Day 326

Day 327

Day 328

Day 329

Day 330

Day 331

Day 332

Day 333

Day 334

Day 335

Day 336

Day 337

Day 338

Day 339

Day 340

Day 341

Day 342

Day 343

Day 344

Day 345

Day 346

Day 347

Day 348

Day 349

Day 350

Day 351

Day 352

Day 353

Day 354

Day 355

Day 356

Day 357

Day 358

Day 359

Day 360

Day 361

Day 362

Day 363

Day 364

Day 365

Conclusion

We're Fucked!